My Path to Math

123456789

Place Value
The Next Stage

Claire Piddock

Crabtree Publishing Company

www.crabtreebooks.com

Author: Claire Piddock
Publishing plan research and development:
    Sean Charlebois, Reagan Miller
    Crabtree Publishing Company
Editor: Reagan Miller
Proofreader: Crystal Sikkens
Editorial director: Kathy Middleton
Project coordinator: Margaret Salter
Prepress technician: Margaret Salter
Coordinating editor: Chester Fisher
Series editor: Jessica Cohn
Project manager: Kumar Kunal (Q2AMEDIA)
Art direction: Cheena Yadav (Q2AMEDIA)
Cover design: Suzena Samuel (Q2AMEDIA)
Design: Jasmeen Kaur, Ravinder Chauhan (Q2AMEDIA)
Photo research: nubhav Singhal and Nivisha Sinha (Q2AMEDIA)
3D Illustrations: Gopal Das

Photographs:
Dreamstime: Borys Shevchuk/Stepan Popov: p. 8, 9
Istockphoto: Blackred: p. 15
Masterfile: p. 17
Photolibrary: Coll-PR Productions 1991: p. 21
Q2AMedia Art Bank : Content Page, 4, 6, 7, 8, 10, 12, 14, 15,
    16, 18, 19, 20, 21, 22, 23, 24
Other images by Shutterstock

Library and Archives Canada Cataloguing in Publication

Piddock, Claire
        Place value : the next stage / Claire Piddock.

(My path to math)
Includes index.
ISBN 978-0-7787-6783-1 (bound).--ISBN 978-0-7787-6792-3 (pbk.)

        1. Place value (Mathematics)--Juvenile literature. 2. Counting--Juvenile
literature. 3. Numeration--Juvenile literature. I. Title. II. Series: My path
to math

QA141.3.P53 2010   j513   C2010-901012-4

Library of Congress Cataloging-in-Publication Data

Piddock, Claire.
    Place value : the next stage / Claire Piddock.
        p. cm. -- (My path to math)
    Includes index.
    ISBN 978-0-7787-6783-1 (reinforced lib. bdg. : alk. paper) -- ISBN 978-0-7787-
6792-3 (pbk. : alk. paper)
    1. Place value (Mathematics)--Juvenile literature. I. Title. II. Series.

    QA141.P 56 2011
    513--dc22

                                                    2010004529

Crabtree Publishing Company

www.crabtreebooks.com   1-800-387-7650

Printed in China/082010/AP20100512

Published in Canada
Crabtree Publishing
616 Welland Ave.
St. Catharines, ON
L2M 5V6

Published in the United States
Crabtree Publishing
PMB 59051
350 Fifth Avenue, 59th Floor
New York, New York 10118

Published in the United Kingdom
Crabtree Publishing
Maritime House
Basin Road North, Hove
BN41 1WR

Published in Australia
Crabtree Publishing
386 Mt. Alexander Rd.
Ascot Vale (Melbourne)
VIC 3032

Contents

Tens and Ones

Haki and Emma play with the toy trains at the after-school center. They put together ten train parts on the track. There are two extra train parts. They have 12 parts in all.

They are learning about place value in school. Haki says, "Look, the trains show **place value**."

The number 12 stands for a number of tens and a number of ones. The number 12 means 1 set of ten and 2 ones.

Activity Box

Look below. How many sets of ten are there? How many extras?

Each number from 11 to 19 is a set of ten with a number left over.

Haki and Emma have put ten train parts in a row.
Their train shows one set of ten.

There are two train parts left over.
They are playing with 12 parts in all.

Blocks by the Hundreds

Next, the children play with blocks. Emma makes a square using 100 blocks. Haki builds four towers. Each tower is ten blocks high. There are eight extra blocks.

Their blocks show 1 set of 100, 4 sets of ten, and 8 ones. They have 148 blocks in all.

148 = 1 set of 100
           4 sets of ten
           8 ones

Activity Box

Look at the blue blocks. How many hundreds are there? How many tens? How many ones?

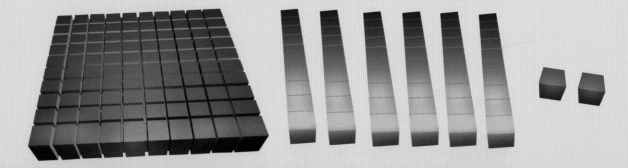

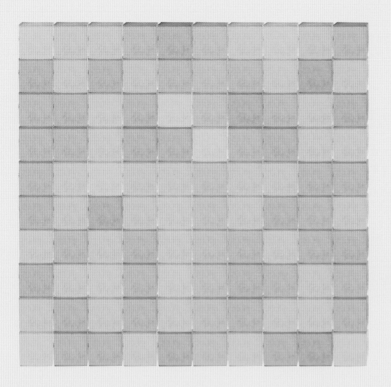

There is one set of 100 blocks in Emma's square.

Each square is a group of one hundred. Each tower is a group of ten.

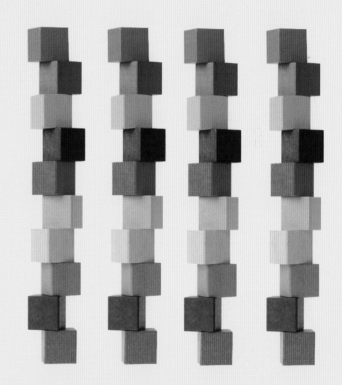

There are 10 blocks in each of Haki's towers. Four sets of 10 equal 40 blocks.

There are 8 blocks left over.

By the Thousands

The after-school center has boxes filled with beads. The children make jewelry with the beads. It takes 1,000 beads to make a necklace. It takes 100 beads to make a bracelet. They use 10 beads to make a ring. They use 1 bead to make a pin. Emma has made two necklaces and three bracelets. She also has made one ring and four pins. How many beads did she use in all?

Emma draws a chart to find the total.

Large numbers can be placed in a **place-value chart**. The 2 is in the thousands place. The 3 shows the hundreds. The 1 is in the tens place. The 4 shows the ones.

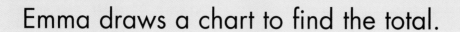

thousands	hundreds	tens	ones
2	3	1	4

Three necklaces = 3 sets of 1,000 beads

Two bracelets = 2 sets of 100 beads

Four rings = 4 sets of 10 beads

Two pins = 2 beads

Copy the chart below onto a piece of paper. Then look at the jewelry above. Fill in the chart to show the total number of beads in the jewelry.

thousands	hundreds	tens	ones

Ten Thousands

Place value helps people think about large numbers. For example, the center has a popcorn machine. The machine pops a lot of popcorn at one time. There are too many pieces of popcorn to count! Yet, you can think about the numbers this way:

ten thousands	thousands	hundreds	tens	ones
The machine holds 10,000 pieces of popcorn.	The buckets hold 1,000 pieces each.	At snack time, each person gets 100 pieces on a small plate.	Haki holds 10 pieces in his hand at a time.	Haki eats popcorn one piece at a time.

The ten thousands place is to the left of the thousands place on a place-value chart.

Activity Box

Look at this number: 84,603.

ten thousands	thousands	hundreds	tens	ones
8	4	6	0	3

Which **digit** is in the ten thousands place?
Which digit is in the thousands place?

How much is ten thousand?
It is ten sets of one thousand!

Other Ways to Show Numbers

The teacher [...]
and Emma [...]
people that [...]

The teacher te[...] the children that numbers can stretch, too! We usually show numbers in **standard form**. To stretch numbers, we can show them in **expanded form**. The teacher writes an example on the board.

[...]dard form: 1,465

word form: one thousand four hundred sixty-five

thousands	hundreds	tens	ones
1	4	6	5

Expanded form:
1,000 + 400 + 60 + 5

Activity Box

Look at the number in the place-value chart below.
Write the number in expanded form.

ten thousands	thousands	hundreds	tens	ones
2	9	7	8	3

$29,783 = 20,000 + ? + ? + ? + ?$

Expanded form is another way to show place value.

Compare Numbers

Haki and Emma play a video game next. Haki scores 6,158 points. Emma scores 6,192 points. They **compare** their scores.

To compare the numbers, they line up the digits in a place-value chart. They then compare the digits in each place. They start at the left of the place-value chart.

thousands	hundreds	tens	ones
6	1	5	8
6	1	9	2

   ↑   ↑   ↑

same   same   5 tens is less than 9 tens

5 tens < 9 tens

The symbol < means **less than**.
The symbol > means **greater than**.
Haki's score is less than Emma's score.

Activity Box

Haki and Emma play another video game. Haki scores 12,250. Emma scores 12,092. Which score is greater? Make a place-value chart to compare the two scores.

EMMA

HAKI

6,192

6,158

6 1 9 2
6 1 5 8

You can use notebook paper to compare large numbers. Use the lines to line up digits.

Number Patterns

Jenny and Mario play the game next. Mario scores 3,250 points. Jenny scores 100 more points than Mario. What is Jenny's score? Make the digit in the hundreds place one greater.

thousands	hundreds	tens	ones
3	2	5	0
3	3	5	0

←— Mario's score
←— Jenny's score

In the next game, Jenny scores 4,075 points. Mario scores 1,000 points more than Jenny. What is Mario's score? Make the digit in the thousands place one greater.

thousands	hundreds	tens	ones
4	0	7	5
5	0	7	5

←— Jenny's score
←— Mario's score

Activity Box

Which number is 10 more than 6,530?

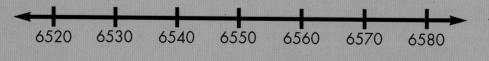

Which number is 100 less than 2,800?

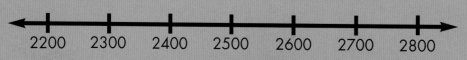

◄ You can count by tens, hundreds, or thousands on **number lines**.

When the game ends, the players give each other a high five!

Add with Place Value

The children draw pictures together. Afterward, Emma and Haki help clean up.

Emma counts 243 markers. Haki counts 141 crayons. How many things do they count in all?

Line up these numbers as if in a place-value chart. Add the numbers from right to left.

$$\begin{array}{r} 243 \\ + 141 \\ \hline 384 \end{array}$$

Add the ones.
Add the tens.
Add the hundreds.

hundreds	tens	ones
2	4	3
1	4	1
3	8	4

Activity Box

Suppose your art teacher has 2,712 markers. Then he finds a box with 223 more. How many markers are there altogether?

thousands	hundreds	tens	ones
2	7	1	2
	2	2	3
?	?	?	?

Use place value to
line up numbers to add.

$$
\begin{array}{r}
243 \\
+\ 141 \\
\hline
\end{array}
$$

Subtract with Place Value

At the end of the day, the children play board games. Kim and Jesse play a game that has play money. At the end, Kim has $175. Jesse has $62. How much more money does Kim have?

Line up the numbers as if in a place-value chart. Then subtract from right to left. Remember the **dollar sign ($)** in money problems.

$$\begin{array}{r} \$\ 175 \\ -\ \$\ \ 62 \\ \hline \$\ 113 \end{array}$$

Subtract the ones.
Subtract the tens.
Subtract the hundreds.

hundreds	tens	ones
1	7	5
	6	2
1	1	3

Activity Box

Look around you for numbers. Look in newspapers and magazines. Look on boxes. Can you find a number that is in the hundreds? Can you find a number in the thousands? Write the numbers in expanded form. Name the value of each digit.

Use place value to line up numbers to subtract!

hundreds	tens	ones
1	7	5
	6	2

$$
\begin{array}{r}
\$175 \\
-\ \$\ 62 \\
\hline
\$113
\end{array}
$$

Glossary

compare Show how one value or thing relates to another

digit Any of the symbols 0, 1, 2, 3, 4, 5, 6, 7, 8, and 9

dollar sign ($) Symbol written to show dollar amounts in money

expanded form A way to write a number showing the value of each digit

greater than (>) Symbol showing which of two values is greater

less than (<) Symbol showing which of two values is less

number lines Lines with equally spaced tick marks named by numbers

place value Value assigned to each digit in a number based on its location in the number

place-value chart Chart that has columns for each place value

standard form A way to write numbers using the digits 0 through 9, such as 4,029

thousands

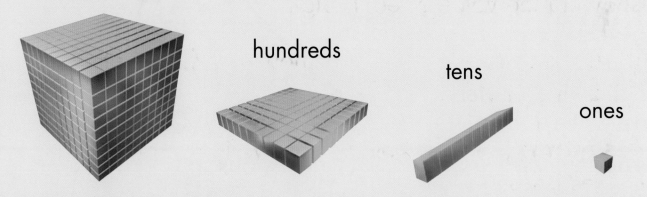

hundreds

tens

ones

thousands	hundreds	tens	ones
1	1	1	1

Index

FEB 1 6 2011